ANOTHER DAY IN THE LIFE

RINGO STARR

GENESIS PUBLICATIONS > FINE LIMITED EDITIONS SINCE 1974

ANOTHER DAY IN THE LIFE

RINGO STARR

This edition first published in 2019
by Genesis Publications

Front cover: Ringo portrait artwork by
Shepard Fairey/ObeyGiant.com

10 9 8 7 6 5 4 3 2 1

ISBN: 978-1-9-05662-58-6

This book first appeared as a limited edition
of 2,000 copies, signed by Ringo Starr

Genesis Publications Ltd
Genesis House, 2 Jenner Road
Guildford, England, GU1 3PL

Fine Limited Editions Since 1974
GENESIS-PUBLICATIONS.COM

Ringo's Picture Book.
Ringoism in book form.
The Essence of Ringo.

For sure, 'Peace' and 'Love' are alive
in this book…

But now a new word: 'Happiness'!!!
Happiness flows through these pictures.
Each of Ringo's photos is so graphically
sophisticated – just framed so perfectly –
and each conjures such a happy feeling.

Hip Hip Hooray for Ringo and this
beautiful picture book of Peace, Love
and Happiness.

Foreword > Henry Diltz

When you're a musician on the road, you get to see many things. Each day you're travelling to a different place and seeing new, fresh sights. If you happen to have a camera while you're doing that, you're in a unique position to start collecting images. It begins as something to do, and then becomes a collection of personal images that can be shared with friends, or made into a book.

Our two biggest senses are hearing and seeing. Music and photography go together, they're cousins. Ringo travels constantly, and he's a really good photographer with a unique eye. He plays the drums in a very succinct way; it's all about the beat and he does it perfectly. All our senses are connected. That's why somebody who's a good artist may also be a good cook. If you're sensitive about things, then probably all your senses come into play.

I know what it's like to make music with a group of friends and to travel around for years doing that. I know what it's like to have an attuned eye, to capture certain types of images that are unique to my own sensibility.

In the Sixties, I was in a four-part singing group called the Modern Folk Quartet. In '63, we came from Hawaii to LA, and that was the year that we first started to hear The Beatles on the radio. I knew a line or two but I'd never heard a whole Beatles song and we were thinking, 'What is the big fuss about these guys in England?'

We were on the road in Massachusetts and we knew that The Beatles were going to be on *The Ed Sullivan Show*, so we pulled into a motel early that night to get a room with a TV. We were just blown away by what we saw. The music was one thing, but we also heard joy and energy and exuberance. And they were playing electric instruments. We were all acoustic – we had two acoustic guitars and a stand-up bass – and right away we thought, 'Well, we're just going to trade that bass in for an electric one.' I would say 95 percent of acoustic folk groups who saw The Beatles that night on Ed Sullivan said, 'Wow, that's what we want to do.'

After that I listened to every Beatles album. The first time I heard *Rubber Soul*, I was on acid. I'll never forget it.

A bunch of my friends and I were in my little, one-room cottage, laughing. I've always thought that it's such a waste of an acid trip to sit and laugh and tell stories. You want to dig, plumb the depths, find out about stuff. So I went up on the hillside behind my cottage in the dark, and sat under the trees listening to them laughing and talking to the mosquitoes, 'Little brothers, I grant you being, but you may not bite me.' I was just willing them to stay away.

I could hear this fantastic music drifting above the muted laughing and mosquitoes. Very much like the cartoons where the cherry pie is on the window sill, and the fox can smell the aroma that comes into his nose. The beautiful music was in the air, and I got up and followed the sound down the hill and across the street to another little cottage. I looked through the window and there was a girl I knew, Cynthia, a go-go dancer at the Whisky sitting in a ring of candles in the middle of the floor. I knocked on the door and she said, 'Come on in, sit down.'

And there it was: an advance copy of *Rubber Soul* that Chris Hillman [from The Byrds] had brought back from England. Now The Beatles were always great, but that hit right into my soul.

The first time I met Ringo was in '66 at Shea Stadium in the dressing room with The Lovin' Spoonful. I reminded Ringo of this the other day and he said jokingly, 'Oh, did we play there twice?' The Lovin' Spoonful had got there early and they were sitting way up in the far side of the stands with monk robes, sunglasses and cowboy hats, trying to be anonymous. Suddenly, a girl screamed and then a few more screamed, and they started coming over. You could see them all coming over the stands thinking, 'There's four guys, that's The Beatles!' And it was starting to be something. Somebody said, 'Boys! Quick, down here! Jump on to the field, in to the dugout, follow me!' We ran down a narrow, dark hallway with light bulbs whizzing above our heads. 'In there, in there! No photos.' And bang! We're in a tiny room and it's the four Beatles, me and the Spoonful. Paul was playing the harmonica and his guitar. John Sebastian sat with John Lennon. And Ringo and I sat and talked for a few minutes. All I remember of the conversation was, 'Oh, Ringo, what do you do with all those stuffed toys that they throw on the stage?' And he said, 'I give them to me son, Zak.'

By the time I picked up a camera, The Beatles weren't on the road any more. Later, I did photograph Paul, because I knew Linda well, George at the Concert for Bangladesh, and eventually Ringo a lot. But never John.

The first time I photographed Ringo was in 1989 for a tour programme of his first All-Starr Band with Rick Danko, Levon Helm, Clarence Clemons, Nils Lofgren, Joe Walsh, Dr John, Billy Preston and Jim Keltner. I went down there with my Nikons and some film and they had the room set up with a stage and all the instruments.

I said, 'Ringo, do you mind if I get up on stage while you're rehearsing so I can get some good close-up playing portraits?' And he said, 'Look, I'm the drummer, you're the photographer, it's as simple as that.' So straightforward, so right to the point, so empowering, so accommodating. That told me everything I needed to know.

Ringo is used to the world looking at him. And everybody and anybody that catches his glance, he's going to give them the peace sign. Whenever I put my camera on him, he puts his two fingers up.

Sometimes, if I photograph Ringo a whole lot, like in Atlantic City, I will be there all day long while the band rehearses. When I get a good angle and good framing and he's sitting at the drums, I keep shooting him, because I'm trying to get the very best picture. At one point, I was using the big telephoto, and after he looked at me four or five times I could see his expression finally kind of go, 'I wish he'd quit that now.' So, I stopped.

He is very succinct and very straightforward but that's also the way I have fashioned my type of photography – quite simple. I have been to Ringo's house numerous times to do publicity photos over a period of several years. He'd say, 'Get Henry,' because he knew it was not going to be a whole afternoon photoshoot, which is boring as hell, and he's done 10,000 of them. He just wants the guy to talk and relate to him and take a few photos. He loves that. We'd spend an hour or two talking and laughing and I could take all these candid photos of him. As a photographer you want to get the real life with somebody.

I've now shot five of Ringo's All-Starr Bands. Once, I was up in Toronto shooting them when Peter Frampton and Jack Bruce were in the line-up. They were rehearsing in a little empty club in the daytime and Zak was playing the drums. I was watching from the dance floor and Ringo jumped down next to me to hear the mix, and when Zak played an amazing fill, I said, 'Man, Ringo, where did you find that drummer?' And he replied, 'In me loins.'

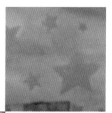

We all have our favourite things to look at: trucks, T-shirts, cows and tattoos are a few of mine. Similarly, Ringo collects photos of stars, peace signs, Buddhas, spoons, shoes, flowers, food, and more. Our eye picks out the things we love wherever we go and when we photograph these favourite subjects over and over, they grow into collections. Once you get into it, you can't stop.

When you're around Ringo, it's all about peace. He says, 'Peace' all the time and, pretty soon, peace prevails. He is an ambassador for peace and that is his passport.

So one peace sign pictured, that's kind of interesting, but when you put two or three or five or ten together, then it's really interesting – you begin to look at the differences and similarities. And when you have 50 peace signs, then that's kind of mind-blowing: 50 people all going 'Peace'.

When I see this collection of Ringo's favourite images, I see many I would have taken and many I profoundly wish I had taken. There is a sensibility of seeing and capturing that perfect frame of something you love and it makes you feel good to save it. There's a spoon, a reflection of a big silver urn, a cat on a glass table, a huge, beautiful grey rock surrounded by dark, old trees. And on the rock is a tiny red petal.

It's amazing that we lived in the time of The Beatles because there's never been anything like them, ever. They were a completely unique thing, the Mozart of our time. When I took that very moving psychedelic trip, where my soul was touched by the music, that spoke to me in my outer limits, Ringo was one of the four guys making it.

And now, years later, when I got to actually know Ringo as a person, lo and behold, it's really this whole other thing that he does that I connect with. He's got this other unique quality, which is the way in which he sees life and captures it beautifully. Perfectly.

> *Henry Diltz*
Los Angeles, CA

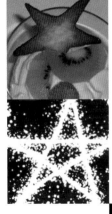

I am a photographer as well as a musician. I love taking photos of random things, and seeing how they all relate.

I love working with Genesis and had so much fun putting together this collection of images, photos taken by me and a few collected along the way.

I hope you enjoy it too.

< Row 1

Blue Star

< Row 2, Left to Right

Starr Drum Head

Starr Black and White
2010

< Row 3

Star

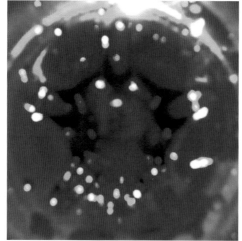

> Row 1, Left to Right

Stars and Shadow
9 November 2017

> Row 2, Left to Right

Man in the Mirror
22 November 2014

A Star for Starr
Hollywood Walk of Fame
10 February 2010

Guess Whose Shoes?
22 October 2016

Of course, I'm obsessed by stars.

Stars, stars, stars…

It's 30 years of Ringo and the All-Starrs.

What a band that first one was, though! Bruce, my lawyer (who still is today), told me, 'Pepsi have asked this guy who has asked me to ask you, would you like to go on tour?' And it was the right moment in my life, so I agreed to do it. In those days I had a phone book, and I just kept going through it calling people like Joe Walsh. He said, 'Levon Helm, Rick Danko and Billy Preston have said yes.' If I had kept at that book, we would've ended up as an orchestra.

I was a little nervous because I'd never done anything like that before. I had three drummers: I was in the centre, Levon Helm was on my right, and Jim Keltner (my all-time favourite drummer) was on my left. We just went in and it took off. We did Japan and we did America; but after a year or so, I disbanded it and got a whole new crowd, and that's how it's worked ever since.

In America, a band can't go back to the same venue every week, but if I change the line-up then we can go back. We're not a band who, like The Beatles, goes on forever with the same people. Nothing has really changed but the members, and I'm always there.

Someone had this T-shirt made for me:
Ringo the Mountie.

> Row 1, Left to Right

Canadian Tour
13 October 2015

Dominican Republic
21 February 2015

> Row 2, Left to Right

Olympia, Paris
27 June 2014

Chicago
25 June 2014

Steve Lukather
21 October 2013

Reading, Pennsylvania
12 June 2016

> Row 3

Recording with the All-Starrs
28 October 2014

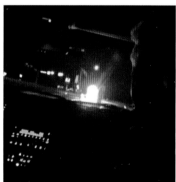

I've got a studio at home in the guesthouse. It's just one bedroom, where the drums and the amps are, with a living room and kitchen. We have the mics and the Pro Tools, and the sound board set up.

I've done at least the last seven albums here. I live in LA and I love it, because all these people pass by, some of whom I've even asked to be on the record. If you come to the house, you're on.

One of my all-time favourite vocal lines was from Ben Harper. He came just to visit while I was making a record. He heard me doing the vocals and said, 'Oh, I think I've got something for that,' and came in. So, I'said, 'Okay' and I put the mic on, and he sang some great harmonies. If he hadn't visited that day, it would have turned out completely differently.

I like to go with that kind of flow. Although I do have to set things up ready for a particular player, we could end up with someone completely different just because they came in for a cup of tea.

Zak bought me this guitar with all the stars. And behind me is a Shea Stadium Beatles poster that somebody gave me. The poster with the car was one of the early acid-influenced posters.

> Row 1, Left to Right

Studio Shot

With Jim Cox
29 July 2016

> Rows 2 and 3

In the Studio with
Amy Keys, Richard Page,
Timothy B. Schmit, Benmont
Tench and Nathan East
20 February 2017

I love making music.
I don't feel like it's work.

If you look back at the last ten albums, sometimes there's up to four writers. There are always at least two. Richard Marx – I always call on him – he's a really good writer and we have a laugh. There's Dave Stewart and, of course, Paul on bass, and Joe on guitar. I just had Rodney Crowell in the studio, too.

I had something I thought Rodney would be good for, so he said, 'Send me the files,' but before I'd had a chance he turned up with a piano player. We recorded two tracks in an hour and a half. We know what we're doing.

This year alone I've guested on seven albums from my house, just from the files. I usually only do a couple. I say, 'Use me or lose me.' I'm not forcing anybody to use me, they may have got another idea.

In the Studio with Dave Stewart
17 March 2014

In the Studio
with Paul McCartney
and Joe Walsh
20 February 2017

> Row 2, Left to Right

In the Studio
with Benmont Tench
31 October 2014

In the Studio
with Richard Marx
10 February 2016

When I was 19 I wanted to emigrate to Houston to live near my hero blues player, Lightnin' Hopkins.

My friend John and I went to the Consulate and they said, 'Here are your forms, go fill them in, son.' So we filled out all these forms and then we went back and they said, 'Oh yeah, that's good, here's the next set of forms.' And being teenagers we just couldn't face the paperwork, so we said, 'Fuck it,' and ripped them up.

Texas must have some kind of pull on me. In '76 or '77 I decided I wanted to go and live in Dallas, because I was a fan of the Dallas Cowboys. I was on a lot of medication then. I went there, looked at some houses, bought a pair of cowboy boots, then flew back to LA.

Rock and Roll Again
19 July 2012

Austin, Texas
9 October 2014

Jerry Lee Lewis is one of my all-time heroes.

Ten years ago, I had the pleasure of playing with him. He's currently making a record thanks to Steve Bing, who is supporting it. And I just love him. We saw him in Liverpool in 1960 when he came to play. He was the punk – Eddie Cochran and Buddy Holly and even Elvis were very nice, but Jerry Lee Lewis was the rebel. He was so great. I bump into him now and then. He's struggling a bit now, because he's getting on like the rest of us.

Jerry Lee Lewis Show, London
6 September 2015

Whatever Gets You Through The Night
29 March 2013

Backstage at Guadalajara
16 November 2013

< Row 1

The Albert Memorial
Kensington, London

< Row 2, Left to Right

Cranleigh, England

Battersea Power Station
London

Rydinghurst Oak Tree
Cranleigh, England

> The Beatles, Paris
February 1964

Albert Camus
French Philospher
1913-1960

Judy Martin, The Beatles
Brian Epstein and George
Martin Celebrating Reaching
the Number One Slot in
America at the Restaurant
Au Mouton de Panurge, Paris
1 February 1964

*I think the Albert Memorial was supposed to
go on top of the Albert Hall. But they left it
in the park and said, 'That'll do.'*

This, of course, is
The Beatles when we
were in Paris in 1964.

It's a lovely picture with the Eiffel Tower
misted out in the background. It was cold,
which is why we all have overcoats and
John and I have hats on.

"Don't walk
ahead of me;
I may not
follow. Don't
walk behind
me; I may not
lead. Just walk
beside me and
be my friend."
Albert Camus

< Row 1, Left to Right

São Paulo View
29 October 2013

São Paulo
26 February 2015

< Row 2, Left to Right

Punta del Este
Uruguay
3 November 2013

Washington D.C.
4 October 2015

A piece of wood. A crab on wood.
And a selfie in the mirror.

Norwegian Wood
20 October 2013

Hermit Crab

Before Mexico City Show
14 November 2013

Glow Stars

Stained Glass Window
23 April 2013

Close-Up Eagle
21 October 2014

> That's My Friend in Miami

There's a saying I always use like it's mine: I feed the birds in my garden because I can't feed them all.

But if I feed the ones in my garden and you feed the ones in your garden, then that's great, and if he feeds the ones in his garden too, that's even better. You can't fix the whole thing but you can do your bit.

I love my birds, they remind me of the human race. Imagine there are 20 birds pecking away at the food on the ground and then another one swoops down, and he wants it all. He's so busy chasing the others off that he doesn't have time to eat, and they all sneak in behind him anyway. He's chasing that one and he's chasing another one and that's a bit like how we are. And look, the other bird gets nothing. So, sharing is good.

With photography, you just see the moment, and that's what you want to capture.

In that second I'm feeling, 'Oh, wow. Look at that bird, how great is that? Oh, I should take a picture.' Even though I know I've got work to do, in that moment I have to stop and shoot the bird.

This particular bird I photographed when it kept coming back to sit on the same corner of my balcony in Miami. It looked like a mad eagle to me. But perhaps someone looking at this book can tell me exactly what sort of bird this is.

< Eagle Friend
20 October 2014

> Look Who's Back!
21 October 2014

Friend of Mine in Florida
21 October 2014

Happy New Year Moon
31 December 2018

> Row 1

Heading for Japan
22 October 2016

> Row 2

Moon in Colorado
13 March 2017

> Row 3, Left to Right

LA Moon
18 July 2016

Full Moon
4 May 2015

Harvest Moon
16 September 2016

If you shoot the reflection of the moon on the water with your phone, you get a white blob because you can't hold it steady. I lean my phone up against things to stop it shaking when I press the damn button.

We didn't know we would have a number one when we came to America. It was all booked months before. Ed Sullivan took a chance, saying, 'Okay, come over for six months,' and it just all fell into place. It was written in the stars, perhaps.

We spent a couple of days in New York and then we took the train to Washington, and all the press were on it. Well, a lot of them. They had actually come to ruin us. They were fed up with these English people coming to America, so they would shout at us, and we would shout back at them.

That's why they loved us; because we gave as good as we got. But it was just us being us. We weren't afraid and we didn't act like we knew better than anyone else.

> Outside the Plaza Hotel
New York

> Row 2, Left to Right

Stars and Lights

Long Time Since I've
Seen a Limo

Even before we landed, I was excited. It felt like New York was a big octopus and it was wrapping its tentacles around the plane and bringing us down.

The incredible thing is, I think I took this shot in the Sixties, but I can't find it. All the kids were gathered and no matter what anyone says, we stayed at the Plaza, New York. I have been told, 'Oh, you stayed at the Warwick.' No, we stayed at the Plaza. This is a memory I won't ever forget.

< Row 1

Madrid, Spain
28 June 2018

< Row 2, Left to Right

Art Park, Lewiston
New York
25 June 2014

Minnesota
16 October 2015

< Row 3

Young Fans Fisheye
27 February 2015

Minnesota: this All-Starrs gig is the biggest I've ever played – 80,000 people. I'd never played to that many people before, not even with The Beatles. We were on stage saying, 'Wow! What happened?'

> Row 1, Left to Right

Zwickau, Germany
18 June 2018

Tel Aviv, Israel
23 June 2018

> Row 2

Tel Aviv, Israel
24 June 2018

> Row 3, Left to Right

Planet Hollywood
Resort & Casino, Las Vegas
22 October 2017

A Coruña, Spain
29 June 2018

< Row 1, Left to Right

San Francisco
2 October 2015

Rolling Stone Shoot
19 February 2015

< Row 2, Left to Right

With Jeff Beck
9 June 2018

Rolling Stone Shoot
19 February 2015

< Row 3, Left to Right

Peace Sunglasses
4 September 2014

With John Varvatos, Jimmy
Page and Paul Weller
John Varvatos Store, London
9 September 2014

> Row 1, Left to Right

Hanging Out
16 August 2015

Drinking Tea

> Row 2

Selfie
4 August 2014

> Row 3, Left to Right

Selfie with Diedra O
4 November 2014

Studio Selfie with Anne-Marie
4 August 2014

Selfie in the Studio
29 October 2014

Being on tour is always very productive for me. I take a camera with me but sometimes I don't manage to get it out of my bag because the phone is just so easy. These are selfies with my son, my friends, Amy Keys…

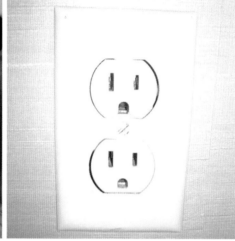

As the tour progresses I begin to see things like a face in the electric plug socket, just as you can see poodles in the clouds.

I love to laugh and my art keeps me entertained. I spend quite a lot of time in hotel rooms with nothing better to do than to take photos of sockets or 'Look at me, let's do another one.' and 'There's a reflection…!' It's whatever happens on the day. But the main thing I do is I play. I play, and I perform.

Another Great Day
with Marjorie and Barbara
10 August 2013

Plug Sockets

Peace and Love Man
19 June 2018

> Row 1, Left to Right

Halloween with the All-Starrs
Austin, Texas
1 November 2017

Happy Halloween
28 October 2016

> Row 2, Left to Right

Ringo with the All-Starrs
17 November 2014

Another Day at the Office
4 November 2014

It took me three seconds to get that face. I didn't have to sit there for five hours for a make-up artist. And here's a little rubber guy in my mouth.

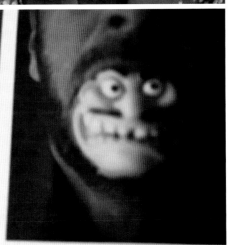

< Row 1

Street Art
San Francisco

< Row 2, Left to Right

No Smoking
24 February 2013

Boardwalk
Atlantic City, New Jersey

< Row 3

US Customs

> Place Card

I have this rule: if three people turn up, I play.

I just banter and talk at gigs; sometimes
it works and sometimes it really works.
I had so much fun at one show. This guy was
late taking his seat, and I went, 'hmm,' and
tapped my watch. He had this terrible shirt
on. It was just the ugliest shirt ever sold.
Anyway, I said to him, 'Not only are you late
but I bet you think that shirt looks good.'
And the audience gasped. So, I said,
'I mean that with peace and love,' and
they laughed.

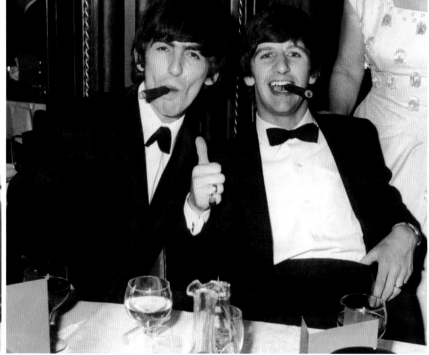

George and me in bow
ties for the première of
A Hard Day's Night in
London. Look at us, we're
just like a couple of swells
with cigars – hey, it was
all new then…

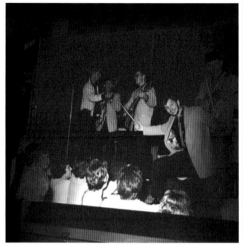

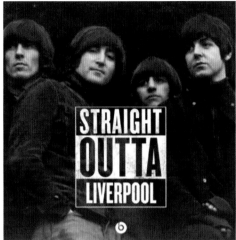

> Row 1, Left to Right

Good Old Days
Rory Storm and the Hurricanes

Straight Outta Liverpool
13 August 2015

> Row 2, Left to Right

Straight Outta Peace and Love
16 August 2015

Arriving in Syracuse
3 June 2016

> Row 3, Left to Right

Liverpool 8
14 January 2008

In Clearwater, Florida
23 October 2014

Straight Outta Peace and Love: that's what it always comes down to.

These top two images were inspired by the film *Straight Outta Compton*. I just said, 'Oh, I'll show you: Straight Outta Liverpool,' which is a similar environment to Compton, and then somebody made these for me. It's only when you get out of where you came from that you realise, 'Oh my God, I survived.'

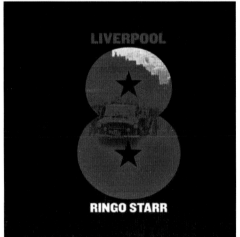

< Nearly a CD Cover

> Very Cool Warning Sign
Italy

I wanted to use this image for an album cover.

It's a piece of graffiti in Italy where someone had put this face on a 'stick no bills' sign.

It was Paul who got me doing the spray-painted Beatle figures.

I had been making these men for years. All of them had been meant as self-portraits although some don't even look like me. Last year I had asked Paul to come and play on my record and, as he was leaving my guesthouse studio, he saw some of my spray-painted men looking out of the office window. He said, 'Why don't you do one of me?'

I draw the shape of a man and then after they are cut out I paint them. They all have a sort of uniform cut. So at this point I had done myself and Paul, next I did George and then John. I showed Yoko and she said she loved them. So now I'm making five sets of the four of us, and four of them will be auctioned for charity. And I'm going to keep one set because I'm the artist!

> Row 1, Left to Right

Stencil Artwork
13 May 2018

Peace at the John Varvatos
Store, London
9 September 2014

> Row 2

Emoji Mosaic

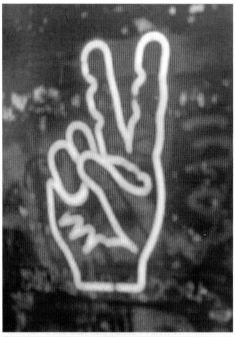

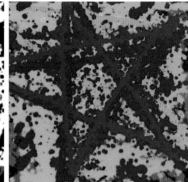

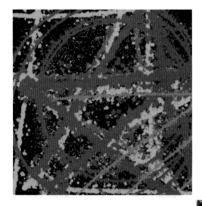

I did a little painting and drawing in the Sixties but it was just odd bits.

I think we all dabbled in it as time went on. John did those one-line drawings. It wasn't as serious for the three of us as it was for John, but now Paul's painting all the time.

I really started in the Seventies, when I moved to Monte Carlo and thought, 'Bloody hell, all the artists come here.' So I decided to get some canvases and paint, and see how it would go. I had a short break from Monte Carlo and then went back to live there from the Eighties. And that's when I got really serious about painting.

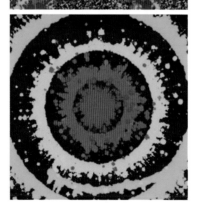

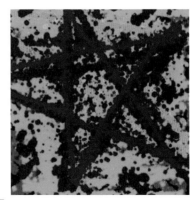

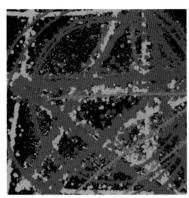 

I create these paintings
on canvas and paper,
and any proceeds go
to my charity the
Lotus Foundation.

I started in '03 or '04, because I was in all
these hotel rooms on tour with nothing
better to do. The original ones were created
on a computer – in fact, I actually started
with Kid Pix. I've moved off it now, but you
start where you start.

I have a lot of apps for painting, and that's
how I do it. I mainly use the iPad or the
phone, depending on where I am.

Starr Spin Art
2010

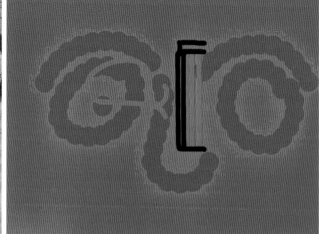

It was through David Hockney that I learned how to make art on the iPad.

Several years ago, I read an article on Hockney in the *Los Angeles Times* about how he makes a lot of his art with an iPad now. You can't draw on the computer program with a rubber or a pencil, so Hockney used these rubber-tipped pens. I thought, 'Get me two of those.' And I've used them a lot since.

The top shot is a piece of graffiti. The head was the part that interested me. The rest is my artwork. I always do the same sort of face, the one with the nose that doesn't have a mouth.

< Row 1, Left to Right

Grafitti

Art
2005-2008

< Rows 2 and 3

Art
2005-2008

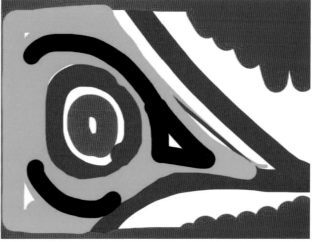

A piece of stained glass and a painting of mine.

Stained Glass

Ringo Starr Art
2011

Bright British businessmen.
That was the uniform. We
had the striped pants, and
the jacket, and we looked
just like stockbrokers.

< Row 1

Floating Hat
28 June 2014

< Row 2

Ticket to Ride
9 April 1965

> Row 1

Ringo Drumsticks

> Row 2, Left to Right

Alpha Television Studios
Aston, Birmingham
15 December 1963

Ludwig Drums
13 May 2018

> Row 3

Ringo Zildjian Drumsticks

This shot is of peace and love with sticks. You won't find a photo of me these days not doing the peace and love sign.

Peace and love are great because they're so simple. I can't force you to be peaceful and loving, because that's the wrong energy.

These are old shoes
of mine from some of
my wilder moments.
('Yeah, big boots!')

Keith Moon gave me the crazy boots and he
also gave me a pair of tap shoes. I loved to
tap, and I even wanted to be a tap dancer
at one time. When I came to LA I had a
lesson from a guy who'd had a lesson from
Gene Kelly. I'm not very good at it. But I've
still got the shoes.

Beatle boot: this was taken as we woke up. We rented a house in Malibu, and this big boot was on the beach.

Beatle Boot
24 August 2017

Listening to 'Tomorrow Never Knows'
26 August 2016

< Row 1

Peace Sneakers
Japan
18 November 2016

< Row 2

Ernest Tubb

Sneakers

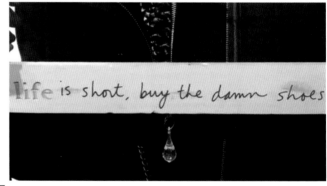

< Row 3

Spot Todd's Foot

Buy the Damn Shoes
18 November 2016

< Row 4

Sneakers

These are shoes you'd need in the car. Look at the shapes and the colours! That's what I love. We made everyone stand together. I needed a foot shot.

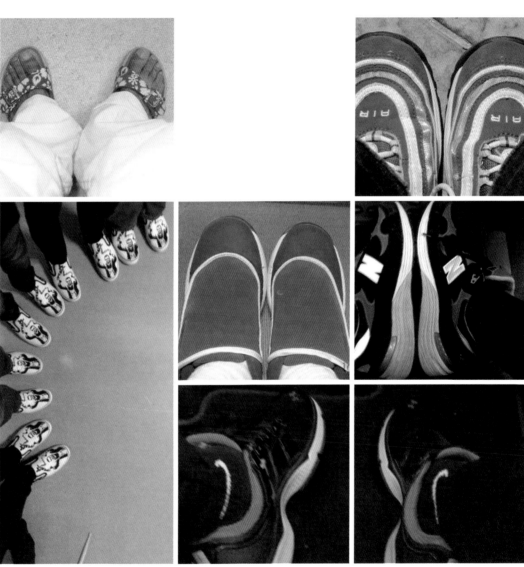

A Selection of Shoes

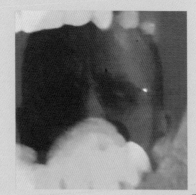

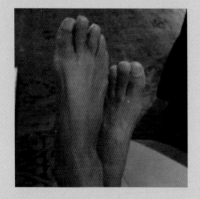

< Row 1, Left to Right

Selfie, Teeth
24 July 2016

Blue Eye

< Row 2

Head Models

< Row 3, Left to Right

Feet

Spectacles
22 November 2016

> Working Out Too Hard

Shadows

This is me exercising one day when I really wigged out hard. The trainer said, 'There's your rib that's been playing up.'

< Row 1

Shea Stadium Poster
Ringo's Studio

< Row 2, Left to Right

Celebration for Joe Walsh
13 December 2016

Rocky Mountain Way
29 August 2015

< Row 3, Left to Right

The Beatles at Shea Stadium
15 August 1965

Shea Stadium Poster
15 August 1965

The Beatles were the first band ever to play stadiums. After us came Led Zeppelin, The Who and many others.

By the time bands like Zeppelin got to play them, they did two-hour sets. We only did 30 minutes, and 25 if we didn't feel like it.

When we made *Eight Days a Week* with Ron Howard, we searched for footage from people who had filmed The Beatles at Shea Stadium. We found very few pieces, because nobody had cameras in those days. Today everyone has their iPhones held up; they don't even bother looking at you any more.

At Shea Stadium, there were photographs taken from a long way away. We found one great shot from Germany and a couple of other places, but no movie footage. The rest was all from the press and interviews we did at the time, and none of it seemed that great. But then we gave it to Ron and he turned it into a work of art.

> Row 1, Left to Right

Joe Walsh's Birthday
22 November 2014

Joe's Car

> Row 2, Left to Right

With Joe and Marjorie Walsh
and Barbara
5 December 2015

Joe Walsh and AC/DC, Coachella
11 April 2015

With Joe Walsh
2 November 2014

> Row 3

Joe Walsh
22 January 2017

Barbara was at Shea Stadium with her sister, Marjorie, Joe Walsh's wife. And then we found out Joe was there, too. So, all four of us were at Shea!

This is the Joe Walsh page; you made it into the book, Joe! That's his hat, that's his car and that's him with a guitar! He is a great friend and an incredible musician. I love you, man.

Peace and Love
12 July 2014

Selfie in Calgary
13 October 2013

Making the Next Record
14 March 2014

With Joe Walsh in the Sun
10 August 2013

A Little Help from My Friends
1 September 2015

< Sgt Pepper
1 July 2017

< Row 2

The Suit Still Fits

< Row 3, Left to Right

Sgt Pepper Colours

Graffiti

Peony

When I was moving I found the Sergeant Pepper suit, so I tried it on.

I was getting ready for my *Peace & Love* exhibition at the GRAMMY Museum. And, I thought, 'Well, I've got it on, I might as well have a photo taken in it.' Which I did. It had been in a box for 300 years.

It's so great how the world has changed. In the Sixties when we made these suits, we didn't really think too much about the colours. Then suddenly in the Eighties, there were comments like, 'It's pink, Ringo.' Yeah. It was always pink, it just seemed like a good colour to go next to the green.

People have named
several stars, as well
as donkeys and dogs,
after The Beatles.

In 1974, archaeologists found bits of a
skeleton that was millions of years old and
it just happened that at the time the radio
was playing 'Lucy in the Sky with Diamonds'.
So they called this skeleton, the mother of
all of us, Lucy. Lucy is your mum too (if you
go back far enough). And that's the story
I live by.

Sgt Pepper
1 July 2017

Every year on Christmas Eve NORAD (North American Aerospace Defense Command) tracks Father Christmas. I was the narrator a couple of times: 'I can see the sleigh now; it's just coming into Philadelphia.'

Elon Musk Rocket Launch
'Space X'
6 February 2018

View of the Moon
Los Angeles

I took this photograph in a garden. It's a digital camera, but I have a great lens and I use it like an analogue camera because I have to work out the f-stop. If I used my phone camera to take this, then I would just get a white blob, whereas with this camera I get the definition. I was shocked at how good the definition is.

There's a space mission going off soon and they're going to put some music on it. They're going to take 'With a Little Help from My Friends', in case the alien wants to dance, and of course he'll understand it.

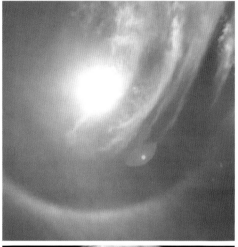

> Row 1

Big Moon Last Night
11 August 2014

> Row 2

Sky
11 April 2017

> Row 3, Left to Right

Flags Fisheye

Our World
Satellite TV Broadcast
25 June 1967

< Row 1, Left to Right

Sunset Sea
7 November 2016

Red Sunset Sea

< Row 2

Hawaiian Sunset
6 November 2016

> Great Sky

Here Comes the Sun
23 August 2017

Sunsets anywhere are beautiful. And that was the eclipse – I cropped myself into the picture.

He Said Love, You Said Peace
22 May 2015

George Harrison
Magical Mystery Tour
27 November 1967

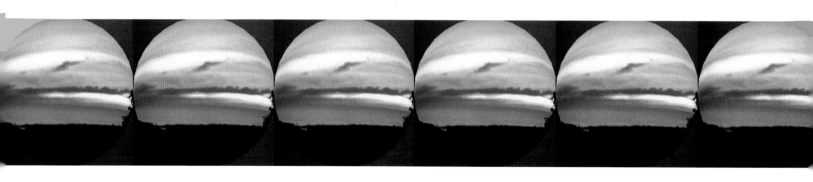

This is with a fisheye lens.
I still have the original
lenses from *Magical
Mystery Tour.*

This sunset is taken with a fisheye lens.
The photographs that I took of George,
when he was doing 'Blue Jay Way', were
taken with the fisheye lens and then I layered
them up to create a kind of prism effect.

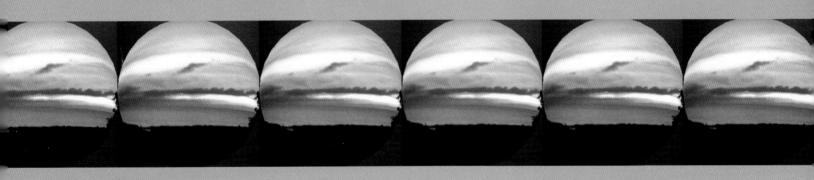

< Row 1, Left to Right

Cranleigh, England

Pink and Blue Sunset

< Row 2, Left to Right

Red Sky at Night

Battersea Power Station
London

Sunrise, sunset. Fabulous.

Back in the Sixties I heard about someone
who went to Antarctica, and every day
he would take a picture of wherever the
moon or sun was in the sky. But then the
weather got so bad that he had to leave
a few days before the end of the month.
Another morning, 'Click.' Another night,
'Click.' And then, 'You better get out;
storm's coming!'

> Row 1, Left to Right

Red Sunset
17 January 2018

Los Angeles Sunset
27 November 2016

> Row 2

Sunset
24 May 2015

More and more people are joining in with peace and love and that's the goal.

I learned from the Maharishi that if you do something good, then two other people will do something good, then three, then five and then a thousand. The whole planet will support you. You're always loved. I live in that world.

The above shot is of Mahavira, the spiritual teacher of Jainism. Jainism is an ancient religion from India. I love it because it teaches you that the way to enlightenment is through absolute focus on peace and love and non-violence towards all living things.

< Ringo Next to the Ganges
Rishikesh, India
February 1968

> Green Glass Buddha

It's Meditation Time
29 June 2017

Peaceful Morning
19 July 2012

The Maharishi's colour was yellow, and that's why I use that colour. Just saying the word yellow is like throwing a pebble in a pond. Those ripples go out and out and out, and that's a bit like meditation.

Say you could take a white cloth and sink it into your mind and your mind is like yellow dye. You sink it in and then pull it out and the cloth is just a little yellow. You put it back in, then pull it out again, and it's a little bit more yellow. The more you keep putting the cloth in and pulling it back out, the brighter it gets.

When I started meditating, I remember asking the Maharishi whether I was doing it right. He told me a great thing: 'You're always doing it right if you're doing it.' If I fell asleep while meditating I'd go, 'Oh God, I fell asleep,' and he'd say, 'No, it's OK. You were tired.'

< With the Maharishi
Rishikesh, India
February 1968

> Yoga Day
6 September 2015

International Peace Day
Jackson Heights Schoolyard
21 September 2015

Yoga Day in London. The building in the background is now the Saatchi Gallery. I was at my friend's place at the time and I just looked out of a window.

Meditation energises me, brings me moments of pure joy and gives me a break from my brain. Sometimes I feel like there are 50 people in my brain, and they all have something to say. There's always an argument going on in there. Meditation brings it down to five people in my brain, and that's the improvement.

We must always bear in mind
that we are not going to be free,
but are free already.
Every idea that we are bound is a delusion.
Every idea that we are happy or unhappy
is a tremendous delusion.

< Row 1

Swami Vivekananda
1863-1902

< Row 2, Left to Right

Gandhi's Words

Buddhist Statue
11 July 2016

< Row 3, Left to Right

Swami Prajnanpad
4 August 2014

Putting Down Pain

Mahavira Statue

'Live simply so others
can simply live.'
Gandhi

The intellectual aspect is, that love sees and understands.
The emotional aspect is to feel as one with the other person.
Love is unity. There is no "me" in love, only "you."
The behavioral aspect is, that love inspires us to give.
There is no expectation; we do not expect to receive.
Such love is wisdom and liberation in itself.

Swami Prajnanpad

Putting Down Pain

The time has come to put our stones down.
For hands clutching stones can't freely drum.
And hearts fisting the past can't freely sing.

George Harrison brought Indian music to the world, because he loved it.
I mean, we all loved it, but George is credited with it.

The reaction was over the top, as if no one had ever heard about meditation or Indian music. The Beatles gave it a great stage to stand on. We did some really good things and we made some good music.

> Row 1

Bird Feeding

> Row 2

Star Decoration

Bronze Buddhist Statue

I love this shot of a tree branch. Every time I walked past, it looked like an animal was sitting there – like a strange deer was watching me.

We don't have this house with the lake and the geese any more. Sometimes our dogs would get excited about a duckling, and the mother duck would fly away screaming to distract them. Those mothers! We had big dogs. But they were like, 'Help me, help me! What's that noise?' Dogs are such scatterbrains.

< Tree Branch

Canada Geese

> Left to Right

Rydinghurst Oak Tree
Cranleigh, England

Colorado

Fallen Tree

The sun behind the tree in this one is dramatic. And the shot below is just a fallen tree, and it looks great. I can't create beautiful shapes like that, I can only photograph them.

I admire David Lynch,
both as an artist
and as a director.
We share an interest in
transcendental meditation.

He has done so much with it. He introduced
meditation classes into some inner-city
schools, and after six months of the classes
the violence went down in those schools
and the neighbourhood.

Now he's teaching soldiers, some of whom
have been shot or lost limbs, to use
meditation to help overcome the trauma
of their physical and mental injuries.

David's just another guy like me who said,
'Hey, let's do this,' and made some positive
moves. He's getting more and more
people involved and that's why I support
him so much.

Ringo Starr
A Lifetime of Peace and Love
11 July 2014

Star Bench by Ringo

Leaves and Star
5 February 2016

A star on a bench that I made.

In 2008 at the end of June, I was being interviewed and the interviewer said, 'Well, your birthday's coming up, what would you like your fans to give you?'

I don't know where it came from, but I just thought, 'You know what would be great? If they could all just break off at noon, wherever they are in the world, and spend a moment thinking of peace and love.' I believe that if we all say peace and love, then there will be peace and love.

< Row 1

Cutting Birthday Cake
7 July 2016

< Row 2

Celebrating and Birthday Cake
7 July 2016

< Row 3, Left to Right

Ringo with Microphone
7 July 2016

Selfie with John Varvatos
and David Lynch
7 July 2014

< Row 4, Left to Right

Peace & Love from Capitol
7 July 2015

With David Lynch
and John Varvatos
8 July 2014

That's how it started. Then I had this great idea to have a get-together. I was on tour in Chicago at the time. We stood in the street giving out little cakes, some of which were on the internet four hours later for $300. But I'm not in charge of that. I'm doing it with peace and love. If you want to just sell it, fine, that's the other side of the coin. I'm sure some people put their cake on a shelf and it's still there.

Now there are 23 countries that have celebrations at noon on 7 July every year. We always start in New Zealand, because they get up first, and it goes around the world from there. Japan and Russia have supported in the past, and for the first time last year we had two little get-togethers in England. One of them was in Liverpool, so God bless you.

Peace and rock, peace rocks, peace and love.

> Row 1, Left to Right

Peace and Love Cupcake
7 July 2016

Peace Rocks Sweet
23 December 2015

Peace Rocks
17 June 2016

> Row 2, Left to Right

Goodnight
20 April 2013

Sunglasses Selfie
4 September 2014

> Row 3, Left to Right

Peace Rocks
17 October 2014

Selfie
8 December 2016

Nice, France
7 July 2018

Capitol Records
Los Angeles

Happy Birthday Ringo
7 July 2015

At noon we go out with peace and love.

We held the same birthday celebrations this summer in Nice. I never know how many people will turn up.

We've held it in several cities, including LA and Hamburg. It just depends where we happen to be at the time.

I have to thank Elizabeth Freund for setting everything up. I have bands playing now, and she brings all their friends who play music. It's so great.

In the Studio
Captitol Records

Capitol Records
6 July 2014

> Row 1

Birthday Cake
Nice, France
7 July 2018

> Row 2, Left to Right

Birthday Brunch
24 May 2017

Birthday Cake
7 July 2016

Birthday – Peace and Love
31 October 2017

> Row 3, Left to Right

More Birthday Cake
7 July 2016

With Joe Walsh
7 July 2015

Birthday Party
7 July 2016

Birthday party. More birthday cakes.

There's one of my spray-painted men behind me. Peace and love.

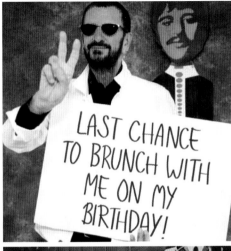

I love Henry Diltz.
He was up at my house
a couple of days ago and
I tweeted 'Hanging out
with Henry Diltz, the last
hippy standing.'

He's a beautiful human being. And I think
his beautifulness comes from his hippyness.
Freedom, peace, love, and let people
be people.

< With Henry Diltz at the
Launch of Come Together NYC
by The John Lennon
Educational Tour Bus
City Hall, New York City
13 September 2018

>With Henry Diltz
California Dreaming Party
2007

Sonoma, California
3 October 2015

Art
2010-2012

*That's a piece of cloth I have hanging
in the studio. I still see people at gigs
in tie-dyed T-shirts looking like they've
come from the Sixties.*

< Olympia, Paris
6 June 2018

Wolf Trap, Virginnia
12 June 2014

Drums
15 June 2014

> Row 1, Left to Right

Peace Symbol
21 March 2013

Tuesday
1 December 2015

Peace Sign
30 September 2015

> Row 2, Left to Right

Peace Sign
30 September 2015

Portland
18 October 2016

Abbey Road Day
26 September 2017

> Row 3, Left to Right

Peace

Peace Symbol
21 March 2013

Tuesday
1 December 2015

We're back to peace and love signs.

This is one of my games that you can play. You've got to get three in a line to get rid of them, and it all says peace.

< Looking Back
The Beatles 'Mad Day Out'
28 July 1968

Peace & Love Bridge, Calgary
15 October 2015

> Sphere in Tree

Circle Horse

Hold Onto Your Dream
11 May 2013

Spherical Window
UK

This is the final location of our Mad Day Out.

It's a photograph by Don McCullin shot through the dome in Paul's garden in St John's Wood. You'll have to ask Paul why he built a geodesic dome.

And this is the Peace Bridge in Calgary, Alberta.

I used to hang things on trees. In fact, I still do.

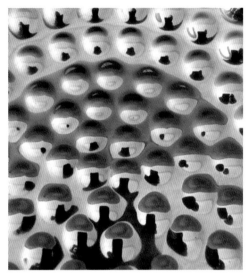

< Something To Do
in the Hotel

Red Reflection

Upside Down Selfie
21 June 2014

> Garden Reflection

Selfie

Garden Orb

Reflections again.

I like looking at clouds. And I think,
'Oh, there's the poodle.' OK, I can
still hallucinate.

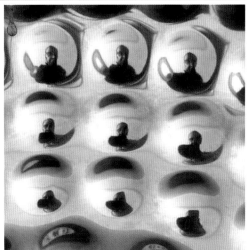

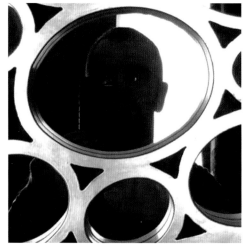

That's me, of course, in the mirror. The background makes such a moon shape, it's like, 'What? What's happening here? Is that dark or light?' But actually, that's my ear.

A spoon, wow! But look what's in that spoon. That's what it's all about.

> Hotel Room Selfie
25 June 2016

Hotel Room Shot
21 June 2014

Spoon Reflection

I take a lot of pictures with reflections in them.

< Row 1, Left to Right

There's the Submarine
2 November 2016

Getting Ready to go on Tour
27 August 2017

< Row 2, Left to Right

Yellow Submarine Fancy Dress

Yellow Submarine
11 February 1968

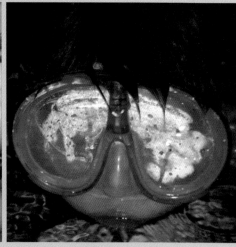

My grandkids all went through the 'Yellow Submarine' phase when they were like two and a half. They would mumble the words, 'I'd like to be...' and say, 'We know your song, granddad.'

There's one of the kids in a mask swimming.

> Row 1, Left to Right

Yellow Submarine, Japan
8 November 2016

Water Inflatable

> Row 2

Ringo appointed
Commander of France's
Order of Arts and Letters
Oceanographic Museum
Monaco
24 September 2013

> Row 3

Yellow Submarine Art
31 May 2018

< Left to Right

Rain

Rain Straight from a Cloud
21 March 2013

Clouds
27 August 2017

Cloudy Sky

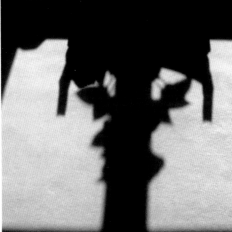

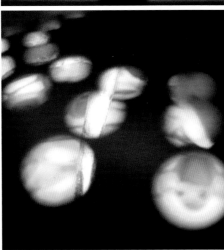

in 10 people now have clean, safe
ater. **Let's drink to that.**
WorldWaterDay   WaterAid

> Row 1, Left to Right

Shadows

Signing Prints for
Photograph Portfolio
London
21 September 2017

> Row 2, Left to Right

World Water Day, WaterAid
22 March 2017

Colour Reflections

We're 65 per cent water.

Someone told me that you can live three
weeks without food, let's say three days
without water, and roughly three minutes
without oxygen. I've forgotten the exact
figures, but I thought it was crazy.

I support WaterAid because I believe that,
if nothing else, everybody should have
access to clean water.

That's me photographing the press. I was at the Chelsea Flower Show opening the WaterAid Garden. It was so well supported.

< Row 1

Press at Chelsea Flower Show
20 May 2013

< Row 2, Left to Right

Meeting at Universal Records
18 January 2015

Press Conference
6 June 2018

> Row 1, Left to Right

Chelsea Flower Show
20 May 2013

Primrose
25 December 2016

> Row 2, Left to Right

Strange Things
25 December 2016

Purple Yellow Orchid
25 December 2016

The things you see in plants. That bottom left shot looks like a little creature.

'I'd like to be under the sea, in an octopus's…' It just fell in. It wasn't something I struggled for hours over, it was just that moment.

I had left The Beatles for a while in 1968, because it was just hell, and I went on this boat that Peter Sellers lent me. They offered us fish and chips, and we said yeah. But it was actually octopus and chips. So, we were like, 'What? We're from Liverpool, we don't eat octopus.' I had a guitar with me and I was smoking a bit of Bob Marley and the boat's captain was telling me about octopuses. That they collect bright, shiny things from the ocean floor, and put them in front of the cave, or the hole, that they are living in. It's basically a garden.

Ben Cort's illustrations for the children's book were great. The publishers tried out other artists who put goggles or oxygen masks on the kids because they were swimming underwater. I thought, 'No, get off. They're just kids having fun in the water. Leave them alone.' Ben understood that right from the start.

< Row 1

Palm Tree Shadows
27 August 2013

< Row 2

Octopus's Garden
29 September 2013

< Row 3, Left to Right

I Love This Shot
Peace Phone Cover

Good Friday
28 March 2013

> Grandchildren, England

Hippo
14 December 2015

When Britt Allcroft asked me to do *Thomas the Tank Engine*, I had never heard of it. I thought it was like, guerillas with machine guns.

Britt would come up with the scripts and we would work on them in the studio. On some days when I wasn't feeling in the mood, I would say, 'Thomas, you little bastard.' And Britt would say, 'I don't think that's in the script.' But I like doing things like that for kids. I like kids. I used to be one.

All these crosses are different because they reflect how I felt on the day I made them. I believe very strongly that is what art is about. I don't have a set way. I wake up in the morning and I think, 'Oh, I'll make this in concrete, I love concrete, or let's do crosses.'

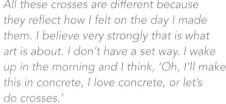

I'd like to say I have a deep, meaningful story behind these pictures, but I shoot whatever comes to mind. This shot is a cross-section of a tree trunk in the garden.

> Row 1

Pictures in the Wood

> Row 2, Left to Right

Wood Carving

Red Flowers

> Row 3

Lily and Rose

That's a garden path at our house in Cranleigh in Surrey, which we sold a few years ago. A big oak tree fell down, so we had to put it to some use. Some guys came with the kind of saw you can use to cut up a huge 300-year-old oak tree and they cut it into all these pieces, which we put back into the garden.

< Cranleigh, England

> Extra Textures

Bad Reception

< Abbey Road,
Strawberry Field
(Children's Home, Liverpool)
31 May 2018

Marble Stripes and Dragonfly

> Christmas Card
26 January 2015

Mexico City
9 March 2015

Who knew the *Abbey Road* cover photograph would become so iconic?

We were sitting in the studio thinking, 'Oh, we need a cover, let's go to Hawaii! Let's go to Egypt! Oh, sod it. Let's just walk across the road.' It wasn't like we set it up, that's just what we were wearing when we came to work. John happened to be in white, I was in black, Paul took his shoes off – we'll never know why – and George came like he was digging the garden, you know? It was far out.

Abbey Road *in the snow. It's a Christmas card. It's great because all the cars are different. They don't even have the Volkswagen. So, God bless whoever made this odd piece.*

They made a cake for me in this hotel in Mexico City.

This red piece is new.
I call it my beetroot doll.

Before a show I always have a baked potato,
steamed veg, and a glass of fresh veg juice
with a lot of beetroot. One time I was
dripping it on the plate and I said, 'Oh, I'll
draw faces.' I always draw faces.

I don't know if other foods are good for it,
but beetroot is great. Watch out for the
broccoli edition next.

The other piece is part of my stencil kit.

< *Love* Cirque du Soleil
Las Vegas
14 July 2016

> Row 1, Left to Right

Beetroot Art

Apple Star

Christmas Eve Flower
25 December 2016

> Row 2, Left to Right

Raspberry Art

Watermelon

Beetroot Juice

Halfway through a show I have a frozen fruit drink. I get a bit of a rush from the sugar in the fruit during the second half. I don't have it before the first half, because I might get too excited or become distracted by someone in the audience and then, 'Oh, I should've been singing the verse there.' If that happens I tell the band, 'Just keep playing. Nobody stops.'

< Row 1, Left to Right

Hotel Desserts
Fruit in a Bowl

One of Those Things

Symbol

< Row 2, Left to Right

Big Love Cup

One of Those Things Again

< Row 3, Left to Right

Looks Like an Animal to Me

Good Morning and Afternoon
5 November 2013

This Papaya looks like a little animal to me.

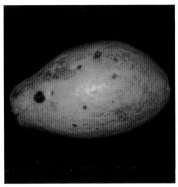

I took the shot of the oil, vinegar, salt and pepper because you can see the stars behind it.

A bowl of apples, again I love the reflection in this one.

> Row 1, Left to Right

Fruit in Argentina
3 November 2013

Fruit Bowl
1 March 2013

Grapes, Apples and Bananas
12 February 2013

> Row 2, Left to Right

Watermelon
14 August 2016

Birthday Cake
24 February 2013

Egg
11 September 2016

> Row 3, Left to Right

Carrot
15 July 2013

Chocolate
18 February 2013

Sunflowers
19 July 2016

< Row 1, Left to Right

Potato Art

Ringo's Plate
24 February 2013

< Row 2

Guess Where We Are
23 February 2013

< Row 1, Left to Right

Dinner
Broccoli

Happy Thanksgiving
26 November 2015

< Row, 2, Left to Right

Apple Pie, Cleveland
17 April 2015

Birthday Cake and Candle
7 July 2013

Food Art

Cake! Birthday cake. I've got a whole selection of plates of food going back to the Sixties or Seventies.

The two things that I have taken photos of over the many years have been plates of leftovers and empty chairs. You can tell a whole story from them.

It's like the movie *Sliding Doors*. A second earlier or later and something completely different could have happened.

> Row 1, Left to Right

Dinner

Happy Birthday, Joe Walsh
21 November 2015

> Row 2, Left to Right

Happy Thanksgiving Food
28 November 2013

Brussels Sprout

> Row 1, Left to Right

Black Dog

Deer in Colorado
5 March 2016

> Row 2, Left to Right

Cat at the Window

Oops

> Row 3, Left to Right

Dog Tongue

Llama Land
10 August 2017

Spider

> Row 4, Left to Right

Dog Nose

Sleeping Cat
8 April 2013

I think it's obscene to shoot a beautiful two-tonne elephant just for its ivory. To kill a living creature so you can have something on your table that somebody has carved.

But you can't blame a lot of the guys who do this, because that's how they make a living and they're very poor. The problem is the people who buy it. We'll be sorry when elephants are extinct. It seems China's supporting us with its ban on ivory imports, though.

When the dodo went extinct (to name one species), we didn't know. If you lived in England a thousand years ago, you didn't know what was happening in Spain. And now we get information worldwide, whatever happens.

My point is: stop. Stop killing animals and grow more broccoli. I'm on my high horse now.

These shots were opportunistic: the animals were there, and I had an iPhone with me.

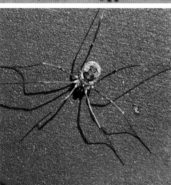

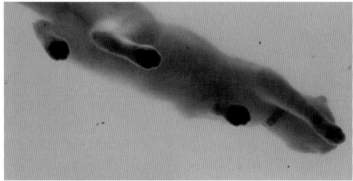

< Row 1, Left to Right

Sweetie (The Cat)
on RS Office Skylight

Happy Easter Peace
27 March 2016

Happy Easter Bunny
27 March 2016

< Row 2, Left to Right

Look Outside Your Window
9 October 2013

Cat in a Box (Sweetie)
6 July 2012

< Row 3

Dog with Funny Face
8 April 2013

> Row 1, Left to Right

Cat up a Ladder

Dog in Daffodils

> Row 2, Left to Right

Dog and Pie

Cat in a Box

Close-up Cat

The cat is just very funny: 'Oh, I'm up the ladder, oh now I'm in the box.'

The dog is like, 'Ooh, I love these flowers.'

This is Easter, in a hotel in LA, and that's the big Easter Bunny.

> Peace Piece
2012

Black and White Piece
2012

Art
2010

< Left to Right

Ringo at the Ryman
23 March 2013

Palms
22 November 2014

Las Vegas Link
22 November 2013

Show in Vegas
14 July 2016

Ringo at the Ryman. I love country music and it was such a thrill to play there.

> Row 1

Caesars, Las Vegas
21 June 2014

> Row 2, Left to Right

Blue Suede Shoes
26 October 2016

Las Vegas Show
Planet Hollywood
15 October 2017

> Row 3

Sentimental Journey
27 March 1970

I only ever met Elvis once, with The Beatles when we all met him together.

They flew me to Vegas for *Sentimental Journey*, I wore a bow tie. They showed me the room Elvis was in, because they thought I was good for Vegas. I had a very nice couple of days and then I said, 'Goodbye, no.'

John and Ringo
1967

On the Lennon Bus
13 September 2018

UK Grey Day
19 December 2015

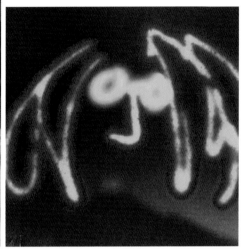

A couple of lads on the
town, John and Ringo,
all dressed up.

> Row 1, Left to Right

Come Together: NYC
Ringo, Yoko and Jeff Bridges
14 September 2018

Peace Selfie
19 September 2014

> Row 2, Left to Right

Chess and Feet

Yoko Badge

We all went to Syracuse
for John and Yoko's *This
Is Not Here* exhibition
in 1971.

It was good fun, Phil Spector was there, and
Yoko had made these buttons.

I provided a piece, it was the only art piece
I ever gave Lennon. It was a bin bag with
a huge sponge in it full of water, because
all the artworks in that part of the exhibition
had to relate to water.

Ringo Graffiti
9 February 2018

John Lennon Wall
Prague

Peace Flowers
8 July 2018

This is the John Lennon Wall in Prague.

Prague is a beautiful city with lots of water and a lot of bridges. It's where that whole thing of lovers putting a lock on a railing and then throwing the key in the water started. We were there on tour when they said, 'Did you know they have the John Lennon Wall?' So, I said, 'Well, shit. Get me a car, let's go see it.' And this is it.

I support Knot for Violence. Which is the 'knot' in the gun.

I coloured this gun in on the computer and then an artist painted this huge version of it. Knot for Violence started way before I joined them. I thought, 'Wow, that's a brilliant idea,' just imagine no violence.

Imagining is all we can do, but hopefully things are better than they were.

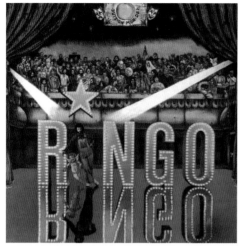  

The *Ringo* album cover is one of my favourites. Klaus Voormann did a great job.

It's got all the players in it. Barry Feinstein took the picture because somebody knew him, and he knew me.

The cartoon of Harry Nilsson and me, with Harry as a little angel, came from a movie script we were working on about a thief who stole all the great songs in the world. Harry and I were going to find them. So, Bob Dylan could be like, 'The answer, my friend, is blowing.' The rest had been stolen!

We were going through this maze of characters and plotlines, and we made a two-minute animated trailer. And that was as far as we got.

< Row 1, Left to Right

Ringo
2 November 1973

Big Brother Ringo

Mirror Selfie
7 May 2013

< Row 2

Magnify Me

< Row 3

With Klaus Voormann
12 June 2018

I did this top image with a phone filter. My *Blast from Your Past* album cover has a similar broken-glass effect.

I love doing experimental things like that. Everyone was against the album cover, including the record company. I was selling a lot of records in those days so to then put that cover out was risky in their opinion, because the picture was just so mad.

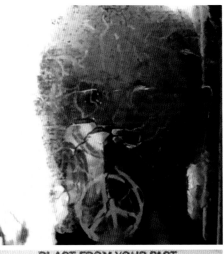

> Row 1

Happy New Year
31 December 2014

> Row 2, Left to Right

Selfie Photograph
8 March 2015

Blast From Your Past
25 November 1975

> Row 3

Tuscany
9 July 2017

< Ringo with Pumpkin
28 October 2015

Halloween Pumpkin

> Zombie at the Window
October 2017

I love playing, it's what I do, but I also love just hanging out with players – so if you're not busy, come on over.

If you look at the credits for albums like *Ringo* and *Goodnight Vienna*, there were a lot of other players besides Paul, George and John. In England, we were in quite a musical neighbourhood. I'd say, 'Hey man, I'm doing this track. Your guitar would be great on it.' And they'd be like, 'Oh, well, I could come Wednesday.' In LA it's more like, 'OK, I'm on my way.' So I find that LA is a better place for me, musically.

Peter Frampton came over a couple of weeks ago. I wasn't making a record or anything, but he had his guitar. So we thought we'd try writing something. We played for two hours, but it just wasn't a day to write a song. We still had a great time hanging out, though.

< Row 1, Left to Right

Heading Home After Rehearsals
29 September 2015

With Peter Frampton
31 January 2017

< Row 2, Left to Right

Goodnight Vienna
15 November 1974

Los Angeles
11 July 2013

Hiking in Colorado. SSHH is the band my son, Zak, has with his fiancée, Sshh Liguz.

You can't beat a cactus and flowers.

> Row 1, Left to Right

Colorado
19 July 2017

With Marjorie and Barbara
11 August 2018

> Row 2, Left to Right

Cactus
29 July 2016

Desert Flower
29 July 2016

> Row 3, Left to Right

Aloe Vera Flowers
14 February 2015

Trees in the Sun
4 June 2013

< Row 1, Left to Right

Face Warp

Surreal Selfie
16 January 2013

< Row 2, Left to Right

One Eye

Puntaca
22 February 2015

< Row 3

Ringo's Rotogravure
17 September 1976

> Face in the Stone

Face Jigsaw

Knot on Wood

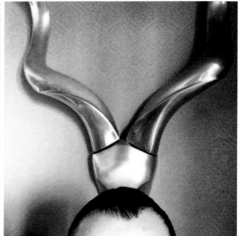

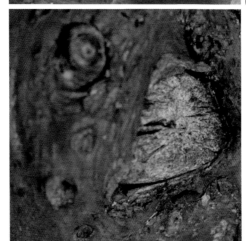

A face in the stone. I'm always looking to put a face on something. There's an app that generates the effect at the press of a button. People think, 'Oh, he must have been up all night.' No. Ding! Got it.

< Row 1, Left to Right

Celebrating Joe Walsh
and MoPOP
8 December 2016

Jet Lag, Mount Fuji
7 March 2013

< Row 2, Left to Right

Japan
23 February 2013

Marriott, Sydney
11 February 2013

> Row 1, Left to Right

Seattle

New York, NY

> Row 2

Bird Posing

> Row 3

In Tuscany with the All-Starrs
9 July 2018

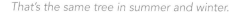

That's the same tree in summer and winter.

I love rhinos and Keith Moon loved rhinos.

In 1974 a girl came into the Apple office and showed me a book of life-size farm animals she'd made out of fibreglass. I said, 'Well, can you make a rhino?'

She made us one each. And then I had the crazy idea of turning my garden at Tittenhurst Park into a prehistoric park. So I asked her to make me a T-Rex.

And she did! A 25-foot long T-Rex with its head up. I never did get any more dinosaurs made, but the T-Rex lived with us for many years. When we sold that house in 1987, I put the T-Rex on a truck and sent it to Elton John, who lived down the road. He's still got it in his garden.

< Hay Bales

Canada Geese

> Row 1, Left to Right

Tree in the Snow
UK

Save The Rhino Sunday
August 2018

> Row 2, Left to Right

Oak Tree

Ronny Under the Tree

< Row 1, Left to Right

Peace and Love
Peace Sign in the Sky
2017

Peace and Love
Garden Statue

< Row 2, Left to Right

Merry Christmas
Peace and Love
24 December 2017

Peace and Love
Garden Statue

Remember Peace and Love
3 July 2013

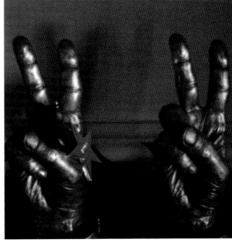

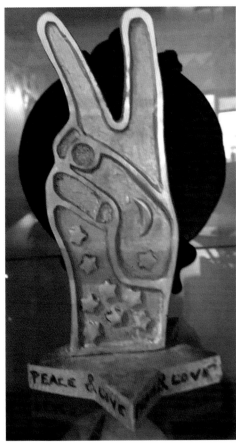

A lot of peace and love signs, all in different places.

Well, that's the real big hand. The first one we did in my garden (opposite). Even the shadows are of peace and love. And that's a cactus that was saying peace and love to me.

> Row 1

Peace

> Row 2, Left to Right

Peace and Love
11 July 2016

Cactus Shadow
20 October 2013

> Row 3, Left to Right

Shadow of Myself
8 August 2013

Selfie Shadow
Peace and Love

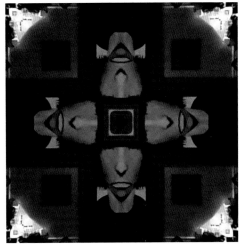

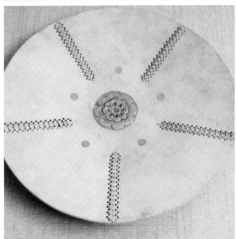

< Row 1, Left to Right

Art

Toledo Zoo, Ohio
1 July 2014

Lucca Summer Festival, Tuscany
10 July 2018

< Row 2, Left to Right

Good Evening, Argentina
1 March 2015

Lucca Summer Festival, Tuscany
10 July 2018

< Row 3

Lucca, Italy
10 July 2018

We were on holiday, and I had been doing a lot of painting with colourful oils. I had a lot of half-full tubes. I put the camera on the floor, and I squeezed these tubes onto the canvas at random. Then I used a Polaroid photo as a scraper and just went round and round. My heart started beating faster as I saw things coming to life. It was primitive.

My Painting

> Row 1, Left to Right

New York
Pink Rose

Birmingham, Alabama
16 February 2015

Happy Father's Day
16 July 2013

Red Rose
14 July 2016

> Row 2, Left to Right

Birmingham, Alabama
16 February 2015

Hotel Window
Room Service Roses

Peace and Love Roses
11 July 2016

> Row 3, Left to Right

Happy Father's Day
16 July 2013

Red Rose
14 July 2016

Stop and Smell the Roses
7 October 1981

Peace and Love Roses
11 July 2016

Rose in Birmingham, Alabama
16 February 2015

Stop and smell the roses.

This is a view of my hotel window. Every time you ordered room service, they brought these nice flowers. I would send the tray back, but keep the flowers.

Dandelion

Dandelion Seeds

I think we've all been
to Alice's Wonderland
without leaving the room.
It's a beautiful story.

Bluebells

Poppies

Spring Flowers

This is Sean Lennon. As I said, I've got lots
of buttons on my phone. If I press one,
it turns into that. I'd like to say I painted
that, but it was just a photo.

I made this mask in 1988. That's how I felt
at the time.

All my pieces have names. So this one would be called 'Chef Alamode'.

< Row 1, Left to Right

Leaving Costa Mesa
20 October 2016

Battersea Power Station
London

Went to the Gym
14 July 2012

< Row 2, Left to Right

São Paolo
29 October 2013

Last South America Show
19 November 2014

Washington Sunset
2 December 2016

< Row 3, Left to Right

Good Evening São Paolo
29 February 2016

Pipes of Peace
26 September 2015

Kept Up After Show
1 March 2013

It's still the same as it was when I started the All-Starrs in 1989. You have to make a choice. And because the band's called Ringo and the All-Starrs, I'm the one who makes the choice.

Usually the hardest person to find is the bass player. So I get that settled first, then the keyboards. The guitarists are easy, because a lot of bands are guitar-driven – so there are plenty of options.

When I'm changing the line-up, I get presented with three or four CDs, with a different mix of players. 'Oh yeah, let's have that piano player, that's great. There's a bass player who sings, yeah.' Sometimes I love the person and I love their songs, but the combination doesn't work. I'm not going to go out with three piano players.

> Row 1, Left to Right

Ringo & The All-Starrs
First Show
23 July 1989

Looks Good

>Row 2

São Paolo at Night
26 February 2015

There's one of my Jersey bulls. He's in Colorado now. One time, it snowed over and all my grandchildren rode on his back. They were all like, 'Come here and sit on the cow.'

Row 1, Left to Right

Colorado

Jersey Bull

Car Covered in Snow

< Row 2, Left to Right

Snow
17 February 2018

I Wanna Be Santa Claus
13 December 2017

That's my hand. It's
in aluminium. Or, as
they say in the States,
al-u-min-um.

I've got a couple of hands in LA now. Brett
Rhodes made the mould for me and then an
artist called Guy Portelli turned it into a full
seven-foot sculpture.

I had this other idea of making a flat hand.
It was seven or eight inches wide and about
three feet across. We put stars on one of
them and a mosaic at the back of another.
Then we made a 'Save the Bees' version
with a big bee on it. I gave that one to Paul
for his birthday.

You can't be in enough places.

< Row 1, Left to Right

Kirby Theatre
5 June 2016

Band's Dressing Room
Tokyo
2 March 2013

< Row 2, Left to Right

Shopping with Luke
13 June 2014

Todd Eating a Bacon Donut
15 July 2012

> Row 1, Left to Right

All-Starrs Backstage
Luxembourg
4 July 2018

All-Starrs Dressing Room
Great Audience, Vienna
20 June 2018

> Row 2, Left to Right

Bands on the Run
8 July 2018

Ringo at Wilkes Barre
14 June 2016

I keep myself entertained on the road by taking shots of the band. It's like, I'm shooting him, shooting me, shooting that.

There's a new All-Starr line-up this year. I usually change the whole band every 18 months, but I had so much joy with the last line-up that I kept it together for five years. We've got two new members now: Colin Hay and Graham Gouldman have taken over from Todd Rundgren and Richard Page.

By the second show we were so relaxed. Graham's 'I'm Not in Love' is one of the biggest sellers of all time and he does it so well with the band, and Colin gets the audience on their feet every night. So, it's working out well.

> Row 3, Left to Right

Ringo with Colin Hay
28 June 2018

All-Starr Rehearsal in Hollywood
28 September 2015

< Row 1, Left to Right

Dunsfold Airshow

The Red Arrows

< Row 2, Left to Right

Dunsfold Airshow

Spitfire

Dunsfold Airshow – we used to be able to
see it from our house. It was like, 'Hey, look
at that plane, that's a big old plane. And
that's a crazy plane.'

These are holiday shots.

I thought, 'Oh, there's a crazy-looking bird on the roof. And there's a crazier-looking bird.' It's always worth spending a moment to take that photo. Sometimes I don't bother. But I'm always sorry afterwards.

Turks & Caicos

Another Damn Bird

Turks & Caicos

Rio de Janeiro
Brazil

Love from Paradise
5 August 2013

> Row 1, Left to Right

Like Being on Holiday
22 February 2015

View from the Window
6 December 2016

Las Vegas
13 October 2017

> Row 2, Left to Right

Rio de Janeiro, Brazil
27 February 2015

Another Day in Paradise
22 May 2015

> Row 3

Postcards from Paradise
31 March 2015

< Row 1, Left to Right

Lifetime Achievement
Grammy Beatles
25 January 2014

With Yoko
Lifetime Achievement
Grammy Beatles
25 January 2014

< Row 3, Left to Right

Rock and Roll Hall of Fame
Induction Ceremony
Onstage with Paul
20 April 2015

Rock and Roll Hall of Fame
Rehearsals
18 April 2015

< Row 2, Left to Right

Rock and Roll Hall of Fame
Rehearsals
18 April 2015

Ringo on Drums

Rock and Roll Hall of Fame
19 April 2015

> Onstage with Paul
Rock and Roll Hall of Fame
Induction Ceremony
20 April 2015

Rock and Roll Hall of Fame
Induction Ceremony
20 April 2015

Spider's Web in Lights
8 May 2017

Spider Web Pattern

Spider's Web on Tree

I think The Beatles' message of love and peace is a major legacy.

And not because I keep doing it, or because John did it. We didn't invent it. Really it came out of San Francisco with the hippy movement. And then it came to England and it was something we automatically embraced.

All you need is love, that's how we felt. And I feel like a large percentage of musicians think that. Peace and love – it's just part of our make-up, to go and entertain and have the love fest.

Leaves and Funghi

Petals on the Ground
5 May 2013

Scattered Cress

Paul is my
favourite musician.

He plays so great and is so supportive.
I have other bass players on my records
too, and I say to each one of them, 'You're
my second favourite bass player.'

With McCartney
20 February 2017

It was great playing with Paul again, and I didn't know it was going to happen.

The band didn't tell me, the crew didn't tell me – nobody told me! We did the All-Starr show, and then I went to the side of the stage and said, 'Come on, Barbara, let's go to the dressing room,' and she said, 'Well, let's just wait here for a minute. Let's see if we, blah, blah, blah.' Then Joe went on. And I thought, 'Oh, Joe's going to play.'

And then I just saw the bass coming from the other side, carried by John Hamill, and then I saw Macca, and I thought, 'I want to be on this,' so then I ran on. What I didn't know was that my drum tech had taken all the sticks off in case anybody else jumped on. So he came on and said 'Uh, you might need these.' And he gave me the sticks. It was a beautiful moment.

Paul and Nancy had been sitting in the back row for the whole concert. Some people saw him, and he'd go, 'Shh! Keep it to yourself.'

With Paul for Love Show
22 July 2016

RSASB 2017

< Row 1, Left to Right

See You Soon, Japan
22 October 2016

Ringo and the All-Starrs with
Joe Perry at Pisa airport
8 July 2018

< Row 2, Left to Right

Give More Love
15 September 2017

On the Road
12 October 2017

All-Starrs in Reno
20 October 2016

< Row 3, Left to Right

Ringo boarding a plane
9 June 2018

On Our Way to San Diego
2 July 2016

> Row 2, Left to Right

Plane on Runway
17 July 2012

View from Plane
5 December 2016

View from Plane

> Row 3, Left to Right

Heading for the Plane
2 March 2013

Just Popping in to See Bangor
8 June 2016

> Row 1, Left to Right

Wing of the Plane
9 July 2018

Mountains

Clouds

I'm currently in the middle
of a madness with stencils.

I've got three stencilling projects on the go.
One is like the yin and the yang man. Each
side is the same as the other, but the colours
are different. This was the first stencil I did.

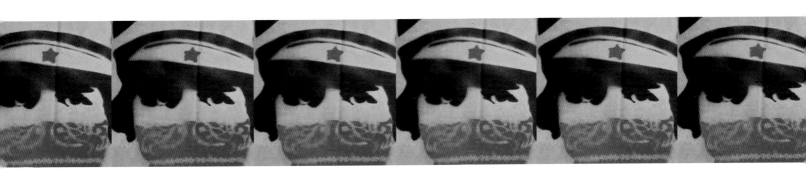

< Row 1, Left to Right

Selfie
4 September 2014

Selfie and Peace Sign
3 August 2014

< Row 2, Left to Right

Turkey
8 June 2013

Yellow Submarine Bike
7 November 2015

AC/BC Bicycle
8 October 2015

< Row 3

Peace Bike
25 February 2015

176

If I'd joined another band, like Gerry and the Pacemakers, or if I'd gone to live in Houston as planned, it would have been a very different story.

But things unfolded. I didn't get to Houston. Like all teenagers, I didn't know where I was going or what I was going to do. And not knowing made me a little depressed. It's a very strange time in everyone's life, because you're not old enough to know, and yet you're too old to be the kid again.

Now I look back I can see that I ended up on the right path.

I'm blessed: I love to play, and I love music.

Great Show in Horsens
Denmark
15 June 2018

Ringo and The All-Starrs
Japan tour
7 November 2016

I love seeing these
pictures all together
showing the different
times of my life.

> Acknowledgements

Ringo would like to thank Barbara.

The publishers would like to thank:
Aaron Bremner, Jeff Jones, Jonathan Clyde
and the team at Apple Corps; Scott Ritchie;
Elizabeth Freund at Beautiful Day Media
and Sue Harris at Republic Media.

Thanks to Henry Diltz, Rona Elliot,
David Lynch and Shepard Fairey.

And, of course, Ringo and Barbara Starkey.

The Genesis team: Natalie Aldred,
Francesca Balgobind, James Hodgson,
Bruce Hopkins, Teresa Fernandez, Sally
Millard, Nicky Page, Alexandra Rigby-Wild,
Marguerite Rooke and Stephanie Luff.

> Photo Credits

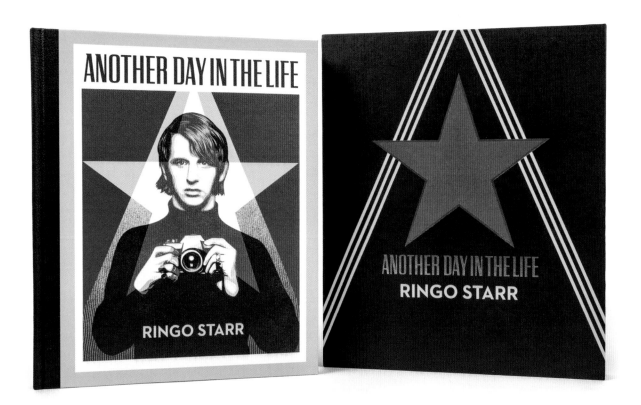

Ringo Starr's *Another Day In The Life* is also available as a signed limited edition featuring a cover design by the renowned contemporary artist Shepard Fairey, reproduced in blue and red, with a black quarter-leather binding and gilt page edging. Presented in a cloth-bound slipcase, each book is individually numbered one of 2,000 copies, and signed by Ringo Starr.

LIMITED EDITION	2,000 numbered copies
SIGNED BY	Ringo Starr
CONTRIBUTORS	David Lynch & Henry Diltz
BINDING	Quarter bound in leather with gilt page edging
BOX	Housed in slipcase
DIMENSIONS	255mm x 300mm | 10" x 12"
PAGE EXTENT	184 pages
WORD COUNT	13,000 words
ILLUSTRATIONS	500 Images

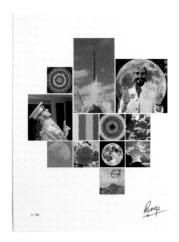

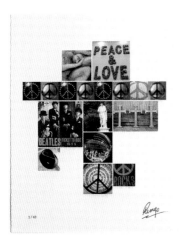

In *Another Day In The Life*, Ringo Starr's first-hand stories take the reader through a collection of more than 500 of his photographs. The photographs, new and archival, are mostly unpublished. A small selection are presented as signed limited edition graphics: a choice of six fine art prints on cotton rag paper, suitable for framing. Ringo's mixed media artworks are hand finished with gold and iridescent inks, and each numbered copy is signed by Ringo Starr.

EDITION	40 numbered copies
SIGNED BY	Ringo Starr
METHOD	Archival Giclée and silkscreen print with iridescent ink
PAPER	Hahnemühle Photo Rag® 308gsm, hand-torn edges
PRINT SIZE	40 x 50cm | 16" x 20"